PRAYER SPRINGS ETERNAL

PRAYER SPRINGS ETERNAL

A Closer Look at the Communion of Saints

Richard France

'Let us relieve burdens and afflictions by mutual love, that if one of us, by the swiftness of divine condescension, shall go hence first, our love may continue in the presence of the Lord and prayers for our brothers and sisters not cease before the presence of the Father's mercy.'

St. Cyprian of Carthage

YOUCAXTON
PUBLICATIONS

To my beloved brother Nick,
whose wise comments, constructive criticism, advice and encouragement
have been of invaluable help to me in creating this book.

Contents

Introduction

THIS LITTLE BOOK is intended to help us to explore the riches contained in the Communion of Saints, that wonderful family which we belong to. In the Apostles' Creed, we profess our faith in it, so let us rejoice in this Communion, and think about our family of saints, always ready to help us with their prayers. Our saints will, whenever we ask them, pray for us. This ability to call on them to pray with us and for us is one of the great gifts God has given us.

We can also, however, take comfort from the love and concern for others that our saints have shown. In a way, we might say that they have already prayed for us, maybe hundreds of years ago. At the time, they may have only had in mind the people they knew. They probably did not think how long their prayers would last when they committed them to writing, or that later generations would read and be inspired by the words that they wrote.

Think of a young oak tree when it is planted in a woodland. During those early years, it is there for those who planted it, for them to look at and enjoy. They can watch it grow. They are unlikely, though, to think of people in later years sitting under the same tree when it is taller. The tree will keep growing and later generations will watch the squirrels running up and down its branches; children will maybe collect the acorns which fall from it, and plant new oak trees in a separate patch of earth that they have chosen. They will probably never think how the original tree started its life. Meanwhile that first tree, which began to grow so many years ago, will spread out, with fresh leaves coming from its branches. At the same time, acorns will drop from it each year, with new generations of children collecting those acorns.

Prayer is like that and springs eternal. It comes from our hearts or from the hearts of those who lived before us. Those who wrote down their prayers long ago may not have known how their prayers would endure and couldn't have imagined how many people living in later years would pray those same prayers. St. Francis of Assisi, for instance, could never have known how popular his own prayers would become. The same applies to us. Do we know whether or how future generations will discover our prayers? Our prayers of today may not be written on parchment with pen and ink but they are recorded in different ways. They are to be found in books, magazines and leaflets, on the back of prayer cards, in church newsletters, even on CDs and elsewhere. Because of this, they will almost certainly be found by those living in later years.

Nowadays someone can write a prayer and have several prayer cards printed and distributed to large numbers of people. However, this has not always been the case. Most of those composed before the printing press was invented would have been single copies, written by the people for themselves or for close friends. Some of these would have been private prayers – the simple act of writing down our own words from the heart to God can itself be a prayer. Also, prayers for others might well be contained in letters, such as those from St. Clare of Assisi to Princess Agnes of Prague, where her prayers for the princess actually form part of the letters.

Many such prayers written by saints were to show their concern for individual friends or for the people they knew. However, many of these have been reproduced for our times and so, when we read them, we can imagine the saint is writing to us, or to a group of people who hear the prayer being read out to them.

Meanwhile there were those prayers like St. Augustine's, who prayed to God asking him to console people feeling weary or sad. St. Benedict asked for the gift of wisdom to be given to people, so that they could deepen their faith, and come to know God better. St. Ignatius of Loyola prayed for those suffering from depression, a condition he himself had experienced. Others, like St. Louis-Marie de Montfort, prayed about issues which were topical at the time; he himself was worried about the plight of refugees in Brittany, where he was working. Most prayers made by the saints have something to say to us, especially when the prayers that they made reflect any of the issues that concern us in the present day.

Still, do we think of those later generations who will repeat the same prayers as those that we are praying today? Maybe those prayers will themselves be prayers from hundreds of years ago; maybe, on the other hand, they will be ones we have composed ourselves. Will those coming after us be reciting the same litanies as those that we are reciting now? Do we stop to think that the prayers we say today may be the same as the prayers of the people who lived centuries before us, calling out to heaven to come to their aid?

When we are praying in a litany we recite or sing the words 'pray for us', over and over again. At the Easter Vigil, especially, in the Litany of the Saints, we might want to reflect, if we had time, on all that lies behind those short petitions that follow the names of the saints. Each individual 'pray for us' might, at first, seem to resemble the previous one with only the name of the saint being changed. It is almost as though we only need to ask each saint for prayer, before moving on to the next one.

That is probably unfair: there is simply no time in the middle of a litany to stop and think about the full meaning and significance of the phrase 'pray for us' or to be filled with wonder on realising that so many prayers will be prayed for us. Our saints will certainly intercede for us before God, presenting to him our praises or our pleas, and that itself is a wonderful thought! So, when we do have time, it is worth just sitting back and contemplating the fact that all those saints have been praying for us throughout the ceremony, as well as thinking of the prayers they might have prayed.

Meanwhile, it is not only at the Easter Vigil with the Litany of the Saints, that we call to the saints to help us. There are so many occasions when the phrase 'pray for us' is heard: when we start with a prayer before a meeting, at mealtimes maybe, in school assemblies, in prayer groups, before a talk, or at the beginning of a journey – the list is endless. We can always ask for help from our chosen saints. We can rest assured, however, that they will be praying for us all during the meeting – or whatever the occasion happens to be.

On all these occasions, the saints whose names we invoke will be praying for us and probably blessing us, too. When we look at their writings, we will find them giving us the encouragement and advice that we need in our spiritual lives, so as to lead us along the road to heaven and eternal life.

Given here are just some of those prayers, blessings, and words of encouragement and advice which come to us from our heavenly friends. We have, of course, many more such friends – with all that they have written or said – than those whose names appear in these pages. There are innumerable saints in the United Kingdom and elsewhere in the world.

Finally, it is hoped that readers will find that those three short words, 'pray for us', can become for them a prayer of the heart.

Our Saints Pray for Us

MOST OF US are familiar with the prayers we pray to the saints, but not so often with the prayers they pray for us. So, in the first section of this book, let us look at some of those that are given.

We are not on our own when we pray. We may be praying for ourselves or for others, but we can also ask the saints to pray for us while we are praying. This way we can have what might be called a 'double prayer.'

The Holy Souls can pray for us too. They are those who have died and are on their journey towards God, leaving the devil behind for good. While on that journey they cannot pray for themselves; we have to do that for them, so that they can approach nearer to God just that little bit more and come gradually closer to heaven. But at the same time the Holy Souls can pray for us, and we should ask them to. After all they, too, are part of the Communion of Saints. We ourselves, the saints in heaven, and the Holy Souls are all part of that same Communion.

Of course, the list of names of saints is by no means exhaustive. There are numerous saints throughout the world and many countries will have their own. Some of their prayers for us have been written down and carefully recorded over the years. Even then, only a tiny proportion of them are given here.

St. Paul, Apostle (c. 5-64/67)

'This, then, is what I pray….. may he, through his Spirit, enable you to grow firm in power with regard to

your inner self, so that Christ may live in your hearts through faith, and then, planted in love and built on love, with all God's holy people, you will have the strength to grasp the breadth and the length, the height and the depth; so that, knowing the love of Christ, which is beyond knowledge, you may be filled with the utter fullness of God.'

∫

St. Paul has told us so much about himself that little can be added. However, there is one aspect of his life that may be worth noting.

He seems to be unique among the apostles in that he had numerous people either working with him, providing him with accommodation or helping him in any way at all, wherever he went. He names at least fifty of these in his letters, although there would have been many more who welcomed him when he arrived in their town or village.

§

St. Gregory Nazianzen (c. 330-c.389)

'Lord and Creator of all, and especially of your creature man, you are the God and Father and ruler of your children; you are the Lord of life and death, you are the guardian and benefactor of our souls. You fashion and transform all things in their due season through your creative Word, as you know to be best in your deep wisdom and providence. Receive now those who have gone ahead of us in our journey from this life. And receive us too at the proper time, when you have guided us in our bodily life as long as may be for our profit. Receive us prepared indeed by fear of you, but not troubled, not shrinking back on that day of death or uprooted by force like those who are lovers of the world and the flesh. Instead, may we set out eagerly for that everlasting and blessed life which is in Christ Jesus our Lord. To him be glory for ever and ever. Amen.'

∫

Gregory Nazianzen was born around 325 in Azianzus, near the town of Nazianzus, in what is now Turkey. Later, during his studies, he became a close friend of Basil of Caesarea – later Saint Basil the Great. He was ordained in 358, and in 379 was called to Constantinople, in order to combat the heresies of the Arians, which denied the doctrine of the Trinity and claimed that Christ was a lesser god. It took Gregory, with his persuasive powers of oratory, to win people back to the true faith, and to establish the doctrine of the Trinity. In 381 he was elected, by grateful people, as Patriarch of Constantinople. Although he later returned to his own town, preferring silence and solitude, he still continued his work of safeguarding the faith through his letters and poems. He died where he was born, in Azianzus, in 389.

§

St. Augustine of Hippo (356-430)

'Watch dear Lord,
with those who wake, or watch, or weep tonight,
and give your angels charge over those who sleep.
Tend your sick ones, Lord Christ,
Rest your weary ones.
Bless your dying ones.
Soothe your suffering ones.
Pity your afflicted ones.

Shield your joyous ones.
And all, for your love's sake. Amen.'

∫

St. Augustine was born and brought up in the 4th century in what is now called Algeria. For nearly thirty years he led a wild, hedonistic life. However, as a result of the persistent prayers of his mother – now known as St. Monica – he was brought back to the faith. After a time, he was ordained a priest, and shortly after that, consecrated as Bishop of Hippo. He was probably the greatest theologian of his time. He discussed at length such subjects as Free Will, the Real Presence and the role of the Blessed Virgin Mary in the Church. He also tackled ethical issues such as slavery and abortion, both of which he condemned, and warned people against astrology and horoscopes, which seemed to them harmless but which could lure them away from their faith without them so much as noticing it. He died in the year 430, aged seventy-six.

§

St. Benedict (480- 576)

'Gracious and Holy Father,
give us the wisdom to discover you,
the intelligence to understand you,
the diligence to seek after you,
the patience to wait for you,
eyes to behold you,
a heart to meditate upon you,
and a life to proclaim you,
through the power of the Spirit of Jesus, our Lord. Amen.'

St. Benedict founded several monasteries in Italy and became the abbot of the great monastery of Monte Cassino, in the southern Italian mountains, the mother house of the worldwide Benedictine Order. He is chiefly remembered for 'The Rule of Saint Benedict', to which both clergy and laity have become attracted over the centuries. Due to its gentle, balanced style of writing and its theme of 'moderation in all things', many people have built their lives around it.

In 1964 Pope Paul VI named him 'Protector of Europe', then in 1980 Pope John Paul II declared him co-patron of Europe.

§

St. Bernard of Clairvaux (1090-1153)

'Let your goodness, Lord, appear to us that we, made in your image, conform ourselves to it. In our own strength we cannot imitate your majesty, power and wonder; nor is it fitting for us to try. But your mercy reaches from the heavens, through the clouds, to the earth below.

You have come to us as a small child but you have brought us the greatest of all gifts, the gift of eternal love. Caress us with your tiny hands, embrace us with your tiny arms and pierce our hearts with your soft, sweet cries. O Lord, hear our prayer, and let our cry come unto you. Amen.'

∫

St. Bernard was born in the year 1090; later, while still in his thirties, he founded the Cistercian abbey at Clairvaux in Burgundy. He is known to many as the probable author of the hymn 'O Sacred head ill-used.' Being an influential figure, he was able to heal the schism between Pope Innocent II and the Antipope Anacletus and his supporters. He had a great devotion to Mary, and also emphasised the importance of 'Lectio Divina' as a way of prayer, which has recently grown in popularity among both clergy and laity. He died in 1153.

§

St. Edmund of Abingdon (1174-1240)

'Into your hands, O Lord, and into the hands of your holy angels, I commit and entrust this day my soul, my relations, my benefactors, my friends and my enemies, and all your people. Keep us, O Lord, through the day, by the merits and intercession of the Blessed Virgin Mary and all the saints, from all vicious and unruly desires, from all sins and temptations of the devil, and from sudden and unprovided death and the pains of hell.

Illuminate my heart with the grace of your Holy Spirit; grant that I may ever be obedient to Your commandments; suffer me not to be separated from You, O Lord Jesus Christ, who lives and reigns with God the Father and the Holy Spirit for ever and ever. Amen.'

∫

St. Edmund of Abingdon was by nature a gentle, quiet man and his appointment in 1234 as Archbishop of Canterbury seems to have been in complete contrast to the life he was hoping for. He is recorded as having hesitated for two days before accepting the appointment.

However, once he had accepted it, he became a stout defender of the rights of the Church. He met constantly with opposition from the reigning King, Henry III. Like his father, King John, before him,

Henry was no great friend of the Church, or even English tradition, preferring instead to listen to ambitious plans of his French relatives, known as the Poitevins. Eventually Edmund persuaded the king to dismiss the Poitevins, to fall into line with the customs and laws of England, and to comply with all the rights that were enshrined in Magna Carta.

Edmund did a great deal for his country and for its people. Very soon after his death in 1240, there were many miraculous cures attributed to his intercession and he was canonized six years later.

§

St. Francis of Assisi (c.1181-1226)

'Lord, make me a channel of your peace.
Where there is hatred, let me sow love,
Where there is injury, pardon,
Where there is despair, hope,
Where there is sadness, joy.
O Divine Master, grant that I may seek
Not so much to be consoled, as to console,
To be loved, as to love,
To be understood, as to understand,
For it is in giving that we receive,
In pardoning that we are pardoned,
And in dying that we are born to eternal life.'

∫

Francesco Bernadone was born in 1182 in the Italian hillside town of Assisi. Being part of a prosperous family, his early life was one of worldly pleasures and a search for military glory. However, as a result of hearing the voice of Christ in a dream, his attitude to life changed.

Later, while praying in the dilapidated wayside chapel of San Damiano, he again heard a voice, this time coming from the crucifix: 'Go, Francis, and repair my church, which as you can see, is falling into ruins.' He then dedicated himself to a life of poverty and, over the next few years, gathered followers who were attracted by his way of life. In 1209 he wrote a simple Rule for them, which was officially confirmed the next year by Pope Innocent III.

Eleven years later a young woman – the future St. Clare of Assisi – came to him, saying that she and her companions wished to follow his way of life. Francis agreed and shortly afterwards they were given the chapel of San Damiano to live in.

In 1224, two years before his death, he received the stigmata, and from then on bore the marks of Christ's wounds on his body. In this way he shared in the sufferings of Christ in the most complete way possible.

§

St. Catherine of Siena (1347-1380)

"Precious Blood, ocean of divine mercy: Flow upon us! Precious Blood, most pure offering: Procure us every grace!

Precious Blood, hope and refuge of sinners: Atone for us! Precious Blood, delight of holy souls: Draw us! Amen.'
'Have mercy, eternal God, on your little sheep, good shepherd that you are!'

∫

Caterina di Benincasa was the twenty-fourth out of twenty-five children, near the town of Siena. When she was six, she received a vision of Christ, and early on in life became determined to devote herself to God and to his Church. She spent a great deal of her time in fasting and prayer, living out her life of faith in many ways. In her early life she worked among the poor and the sick.

Over time, she wrote several letters to prominent people, persuading them to reform the Church and to stay loyal to the Pope. She even wrote to the Pope himself, encouraging him in his role as head of the Universal Church.

However, Catherine of Siena is best known for her 'Dialogue of Divine Providence', a conversation with Jesus. She became ever more closely united with her Lord, dying at the age of thirty-three, the same age as Jesus himself was when he was crucified and when he rose again.

§

St. Ignatius of Loyola (1491-1556)

'O Christ Jesus, when all is darkness and we feel our weakness and helplessness, give us the sense of your presence, your love, your strength. Help us to have perfect trust in your protecting love and strengthening power, so that nothing may frighten or worry us for, living close to you, we shall see your hand, your purpose, your will through all things.'

∫

Inigo Lopez de Loyola was born in the Basque village of Loyola, in 1491. At the age of twenty-six, he became a soldier, and may have expected have a long military career. However, after six years, he was badly wounded and was taken back to the castle – where his family lived — at Loyola. There, having found no secular books about soldiering or similar, he found himself reading about the service that the saints had rendered to God (never imagining that he would become one himself one day).

Following that he went on a pilgrimage to the Spanish shrine at Montserrat, and then to Manresa, where he started writing his famous book *The Spiritual Exercises*. After this came several years of study, during which time he gathered a small band of followers, including the future St. Francis Xavier. In 1539, together with them, he founded the Society of Jesus, becoming its first superior-general, and his Society was approved by Pope Paul III the following year. St. Ignatius died in Rome, in the year 1556.

§

St. Louis Marie de Montfort (1673-1716)

'O Jesus, You who in the very first days of your earthly life were compelled, together with Mary, your loving Mother, and Saint Joseph, to leave your native land and to endure in Egypt the misery and discomforts of poor refugees, turn your eyes upon our brothers and sisters who, far away from their country and from all that is dear to them, are often forced to struggle with the difficulties of a new life, and are likewise often exposed to grave dangers and snares for their immortal souls.

Be their guide in their uncertain journey, their help in trouble, their comfort in sorrow; keep them safe in their faith, holy in their lives, and faithful to their children, their wives, and their parents: grant, O Lord, that we may be able to embrace them affectionately once more in their native land, and hereafter to live inseparably united to them at the foot of your throne in our heavenly country. Amen.'

St. Louis Marie de Montfort was born in 1673, in the town of Montfort-sur-Meu. After studying for the priesthood, he was ordained in 1701, beginning his work on parish missions among the poor. It was there that he formed a strong devotion to the Blessed Virgin Mary. He then became hospital chaplain in Poitiers and began to organise retreats, while working on more parish missions, encouraging and reinforcing people's faith and calling them to renew their baptismal promises. Such parish missions were to form a major part of his work.

In 1703 he formed 'The Company of Mary', better known now as 'The Montfort Fathers', to join him in carrying out this work. Two years later he founded 'The Daughters of Wisdom', who would care for the destitute and the poor.

His greatest legacy to the world, however, must be his True Devotion to Mary, written in 1712 and, slightly less well-known, The Secret of the Rosary, and his thirty-three-day Total Consecration to Mary. He died aged forty-three, in 1716, at Saint Laurent-sur-Sevre.

§

St. John Vianney (1786-1859)

'God, please give to your Church today many more priests after your own heart.

May they be worthy representatives of Christ the Good Shepherd.

May they wholeheartedly devote themselves to prayer and penance; be examples of humility and poverty; shining models of holiness, tireless and powerful preachers of the Word of God; zealous dispensers of your grace in the sacraments.

May their loving devotion to your Son Jesus in the Eucharist, and to Mary his mother, be the twin fountains of fruitfulness for their ministry'.

∫

Jean-Marie Vianney was born in the year 1786 in the village of Dardilly, near Lyon. He was ordained priest in 1815, and three years later was sent to Ars, a tiny village far from anywhere. It was regarded by the clergy at that time as being unimportant and therefore would be just right for a priest like Jean-Marie, who couldn't understand or speak Latin, except sufficient to say Mass. Knowing Latin was a prerequisite for ordination in those days.

However, wonderful things were to happen in his parish. He had a tremendous influence on the people there, who before his arrival had led a carefree, pagan life. He renewed and strengthened their faith and became known for spending the night in prayer, face down on the floor of his church, praying for them, in addition to the long hours he would spend hearing their confessions.

In fact, the time he spent in the confessional brought him closer to God. and to his parishioners. Soon thousands started coming to him, seeking spiritual guidance or to repent of their sins. Even a new railway line was built in order to bring people to him, to have their confessions heard by him.

After a long, fulfilled life he died in 1859. Over six thousand people were at his funeral.

§

St. Elizabeth of the Trinity (1880-1906)

'I am praying fervently for you, that God may invade all the powers of your soul, that He may make you live

in communion with His whole mystery, that everything in you may be divine and marked with His seal, so that you may be another Christ working for the glory of the Father! I want to work for the glory of God, and for that I must be wholly filled with Him; then I will be all-powerful: one look, one desire will become an irresistible prayer than can obtain everything, since it is, so to speak, God whom we are offering to God.

May our souls be one in Him, and while you bring Him to souls, I will remain like Mary Magdalene, silent and adoring, close to the Master, asking Him to make your word fruitful in souls.'

∫

Élizabeth Catez was born in the French town of Dijon on 18 July 1880. After her father's death in 1887, the family moved to the town of Dijon and it was during her time there that she developed a profound understanding of the Trinity, forming a devotion to it. She passed her time visiting the sick, singing in the church choir and teaching religion to children, who had to become factory-workers, since they needed to add to the family income. On 2 August 1901 Elizabeth entered the local convent where she became a Discalced Carmelite nun.

At the end of her life, she said: 'I think that in Heaven my mission will be to draw souls by helping them to go out of themselves in order to cling to God by a wholly simple and loving movement, and to keep them in this great silence which will allow God to communicate Himself to them and to transform them into Himself.'

Her spirituality is considered to be remarkably similar to that of her contemporary and compatriot and Discalced Carmelite sister, Thérèse of Lisieux, who was cloistered at the Carmel in Lisieux; the two shared a zeal for contemplation and the salvation of souls. She died on 9th November 1906. Elizabeth of the Trinity was beatified by Pope John Paul on 25th November 1984 and canonized by Pope Francis on 16th October 2016.

§

St. Faustina (1905-1938)

'I want to be completely transformed into Your mercy and to be Your living reflection, O Lord. May the greatest of all divine attributes, that of Your unfathomable mercy, pass through my heart and soul to my neighbour.

Help me, O Lord, that my eyes may be merciful, so that I may never suspect or judge from appearances, but look for what is beautiful in my neighbours' souls and come to their rescue.

Help me, that my ears may be merciful, so that I may give heed to my neighbours' needs and not be indifferent to their pains and moanings.

Help me, O Lord, that my tongue may be merciful, so that I should never speak negatively of my neighbour but have a word of comfort and forgiveness for all.

Help me, O Lord, that my hands may be merciful and filled with good deeds, so that I may do only good to my neighbours and take upon myself the more difficult and toilsome tasks.

Help me, O Lord, that my feet may be merciful, so that I may hurry to assist my neighbour, overcoming my own fatigue and weariness. My true rest is in the service of my neighbour.

Help me, O Lord, that my heart may be merciful so that I myself may feel all the sufferings of my neighbour. I will refuse my heart to no one. I will be sincere even with those who, I know, will abuse my kindness. And I will lock myself up in the most merciful Heart of Jesus. I will bear my own suffering in silence. May Your mercy, O Lord, rest upon me.'

∫

Helena Kowalska was born in Poland in 1905 and at the age of nineteen had a vision of the suffering Christ. She straightaway decided to join the Congregation of the Sisters of Our Lady of Mercy, where she took the name of Sister Maria Faustina of the Most Blessed Sacrament. While there she received several visions of Jesus, in which he spoke to her at length of the extent of his mercy. When he appeared to her, he was dressed in a white garment, with red and white rays radiating from his heart. He then told her to paint an image of himself, exactly as she saw him, with the words underneath 'Jesus, I Trust in You.' Her confessor, Fr. Michael Sopocko, then advised her to record all the words that Jesus spoke to her in a diary. It is now known simply as 'The Diary', the full title being 'Divine Mercy in my Soul.'

Like St. Catherine of Siena before her, she too died at thirty-three, the age Jesus had been when he himself died and rose again to life.

§

Pope St. John Paul II (1920-2005)

'Heavenly Father, we praise you and we thank you for the gift of family life.

Grant through your Son, Jesus Christ, born of a woman, that every family may become for each successive generation a place of life and love.

Grant that your grace may guide the thoughts and actions of husbands and wives for the good of their families and all the families of the world.

Grant that the young may find in the family a solid support for their human dignity and for their growth in faith and love.

Grant that all who believe in your Son may proclaim the importance of the family with honesty and truth.

Grant that love, strengthened by the sacrament of marriage, may prove mightier than all the weakness and trials through which our families sometimes pass. Inspire all leaders of Church and State to know more clearly that it is in marriage and family life that we know your presence and love in a special way.

May your name be held holy and may your kingdom be established in our world. We make all our prayers through Christ our Lord. Amen.'

∫

Karol Wojtyla was born in Poland in 1920. During his late teens and early twenties, he had various jobs, became involved in acting and also worked as a playwright. However, in 1939 after the Nazis had invaded and occupied Poland, he began studying for the priesthood, attending the underground seminary which had been set up – the Nazis were trying to destroy any form of Polish culture. After the war and the end of the Nazi Occupation, the Poles breathed a sigh of relief – only to find that the Soviet Occupation had replaced the Nazi Occupation. Fr. Wojtyla, as he was now, managed to look after the spiritual lives of those in his charge, though with great care, because of the constant dangers which existed.

Nevertheless, he continued to resist the Soviet authorities and in 1958 he became auxiliary bishop of Krakow, and in 1963 Archbishop.

In 1978 he was elected pope, taking the name John Paul, and the following year he visited his home country of Poland. His rousing speech to the people of Poland brought about the creation of a trade union, 'Solidarnosc.' At the same time his negotiations with the leaders of Poland were instrumental in bringing about the fall of Communism in Poland and, eventually, in the rest of Eastern Europe.

During his long pontificate, he visited 129 countries, re-invigorating the Catholic faith wherever he went. He worked hard to improve relations with other faiths, reaching out to the Jews, to Muslims and to the Orthodox churches. He also consolidated and clarified the teaching of the Church, bringing it all together in the *Catechism of the Catholic Church*, which was published in 1992. Easy-to-read and widely available, it is one of his lasting legacies to us. Pope John Paul died in 2002, and a few years afterwards he was canonized as Pope St. John Paul II.

Our Saints Bless Us

DO OUR SAINTS just pray for us? Surely, after praying for us, they bless us, too. After all, it is only natural that they follow their prayer for us with a blessing.

The word blessing, as used here, is not necessarily a liturgical blessing but simply a form of words which speak to a person's soul. Most of the prayers and blessings belonging to our saints are unknown. A few, however, have come down to us.

Some blessings are longer than others. They are sometimes pure blessing, like that of St. Francis of Assisi, though occasionally they are much longer. For example, those given by St. Clare of Assisi in her letters would have contained, as well as the blessing, an encouragement to live a virtuous life, and to remain faithful to the Lord.

Blessings come in many forms. In the past, like prayers, they could sometimes form part of the letters written by people to their friends. Blessings, like prayers, are evergreen: just think of the famous one which comes at the end of the *Book of Numbers*, 'The Lord bless you and keep you.' That particular blessing may be several thousand years old, and yet it is widely used today and has even been set to music. It was adapted by St. Francis of Assisi for the monks in his monastery, and that adaptation is given here. Then there is the blessing of St. Aelred of Rievaulx – the demonstration of his love and concern for his sister, found in one of his letters. It would have been meant, at the time, just for her. Now, however, the same blessing can be given again to us, or to whoever reads or hears the blessing.

Then there are much shorter blessings, like that of St. John of the Cross, which was simply 'Jesus be in your soul', awakening in the other person the presence and love of God within them. Or that of St. Catherine of Siena, 'Dwell in God's sweet love', inviting them to make their home in God. Let us, imagine that St. Catherine is speaking to us too and inviting us to make our home in God.

§

St. Columba (6th century)

'May the fire of God's love burn brightly and steadfastly in our hearts like the golden light within the sanctuary lamp. See that you be at peace among yourselves, my children, and love one another. Follow the example of good men of old, and God will comfort you and help you, both in this world and in the world which is to come. Amen.'

∫

St. Columba was an Irish Missionary who lived in the 6th century. Much of his life was spent founding monasteries.

Throughout the land, there were individuals who had withdrawn into the countryside to live a quiet life of prayer. They lived in cells in the woodland or in caves, often near each other, with a chapel or oratory where they could meet together once a week. Such disparate groupings of men or women in Ireland would have sought out the local bishop to ask him to give them a Rule. Then the Rule that he gave them would provide them with guidelines for a way of life which would bind them together as a community, with a set time for prayer, meals, etc. The bishop would then organise the building of a place where they could live and pray together, which in time became known as a monastery.

It was in this way that Bishop Columba founded monasteries and convents throughout Ireland. The most famous of these, however, was built when he later crossed the seas in a large coracle – a boat made of wood with a leather covering stretched over the hull – to take the message of Christianity to Scotland. It was here, on the Hebridean Isle of Iona, that he founded the Abbey which will forever be associated with him.

§

St. Aelred of Rievaulx (1110-1167)

'Let there be no imaginable trouble in the days to come that could make you afraid, but let all your trust and hope be in Him who feeds the birds of the air and arrays the lilies and flowers of the field with more beauty than Solomon ever had in all his finery.

Let Him be your storehouse; let Him be your gold purse, your riches and all your delight and pleasure. Let Him be everything to you in all your needs, who is blessed for ever and ever. Amen.'

∫

Saint Aelred lived in the 12th century and was for some time Master of the Royal Household of King David of Scotland. However, he turned his back on a life which would have offered him fame and prosperity, and joined the Cistercian Abbey of Rievaulx, on the edge of the North Yorkshire Moors. He was later elected abbot, and many spoke of his loving and caring attitude towards the monks there. He is mainly known as a writer of spiritual books, the more famous ones being *Spiritual Friendship* and *The Mirror of Charity*.

§

St. Francis of Assisi (1181/82 - 1226)

'The Lord bless you and keep you.
May He show His face to you and have mercy.
May He turn His countenance to you and give you peace.
The Lord bless you!'

∫

'The Lord give you peace.'

∫

'Blessed is that religious who feels no pleasure or joy save in most holy conversation and the works of the Lord, and who by these means leads men to the love of God in joy and gladness.'

§

St. Clare of Assisi (1194-1253)

'I bless you in my life and after my death, as much as I can and even more than I can, with all the blessings with which the Father of mercies has blessed and will bless in heaven and on earth his sons and daughters, and with which a spiritual father and a spiritual mother

have blessed and will bless their spiritual sons and daughters. Amen.'

∫

Chiara Offreducio was born in Assisi in 1194. At the age of eighteen, she turned her back on her wealthy family, Clare was inspired by the preaching of Francis of Assisi to join him. In 1216, in San Damiano near Assisi she founded the Order which became known as the Poor Clares.

She is probably best known for giving us an example of the power of the Eucharist. When the soldiers of the Emperor Frederick II were attacking the convent, Clare, despite being ill at the time, had herself carried outside to the gate of the convent where she held up a monstrance containing the Blessed Host, and the attackers straightaway retreated. Paintings and statues of her often show her with a monstrance. She died in 1253, at San Damiano.

§

St. Catherine of Siena (1347 -1380)

'Dwell in God's sweet love.'

§

St. John of the Cross (1542-1591)

'Jesus be in your soul.'

∫

'May God grant you his Spirit.'

John of the Cross was born in the Spanish town of Fontiveros, in 1542. After his education he worked in a hospital, and when he was twenty-four he was ordained as a Carmelite Friar. Shortly after his ordination he met Teresa of Avila, who shared with him her plans for a much-needed reform of the Carmelite Order and for a new branch of the Order to be known as the 'Discalced Carmelites.' The idea was for a new group of monasteries which would allow more time for prayer and contemplation and be more disciplined. Teresa would found convents for the women and John would set up monasteries for the men. John founded the first monastery in 1568, despite the growing tension between the Discalced and the Calced, which event led to his own imprisonment. (The word 'Calced' referred to 'those with shoes.' Shoes were a sign of wealth and comfort).

It was at this time that John adopted the title 'of the Cross' which replaced his former title of 'St. Matthias', to mark the new start in his life as a Carmelite friar.

He is perhaps best known for his poems including, among others, 'The Dark Night of the Soul', describing the crisis of faith which some Christians experience on their journey to God. He was gradually given more responsibilities and, finally, made Vicar-General of the Carmelite province of Andalusia, where he died in 1591.

§

St. Pius of Pietrelcina (1887-1968)

'May Jesus comfort you in all your afflictions.

May He sustain you in dangers, watch over you always with His grace, and indicate the safe path that leads to eternal salvation.

And may He render you always dearer to His Divine Heart and always more worthy of Paradise. Amen.'

Francesco Forgione was born to Giuseppa and Grazio Forgione, in the small farming town of Pietrelcina, Italy on May 25, 1887. On August 10, 1910, at the age of twenty-three, Padre Pio – as he came to be known - was ordained to the priesthood. The celebration of the Holy Mass was, for Padre Pio, the centre of his spirituality. Due to the long pauses of contemplative silence into which he entered at various times during it, his Mass could sometimes last several hours. Everything about him spoke of how intensely he was living the Passion of Christ.

He also used to say that he had a special mission to the souls in Purgatory and encouraged everyone to pray for them, saying, 'We must empty Purgatory with our prayers!'

Shortly after his ordination, he wrote a letter to his spiritual director, Father Benedetto Nardella, in which he asked permission to offer his life as a victim for sinners. He wrote, 'For a long time I have felt in myself a need to offer myself to the Lord as a victim for poor sinners and for the souls in Purgatory. This desire has been growing continually in my heart so that it has now become what I would call a strong passion. It seems to me that Jesus wants this.'

When Padre Pio was thirty-one, the wounds of Christ, the stigmata, appeared on his hands and feet. This happened on Friday, September 20, 1918, after Mass, while he was praying before a crucifix.

In addition, God endowed him with many extraordinary spiritual gifts and charisms, the gift of conversions, and the grace to see angelic beings in form. There was also a fragrance which emanated from his wounds; even today, long after his death, people talk about this fragrance, sometimes referring to it as 'Padre Pio's Roses', a sign of his sudden but welcome entry into their lives.

Like St. John Vianney before him, Padre Pio became specially known for the time he spent hearing confessions. Thousands of men and women returned to the practice of their faith after going to confession to him. He died on September 23, 1968 at the age of eighty-one. Even after his death, his work seemed to continue and 'Padre Pio Prayer Groups' were constantly being formed.

Pope John Paul II canonized him on June 16, 2002.

Our Saints Encourage Us

IT IS REASSURING, when doing any work or travelling anywhere, to have a guide, someone who has experience of the work or who has travelled on the same road. Then we can see how necessary it is to start from the right place and to have the right attitude. Having someone to teach us how to have the correct mindset, who can help us to see things from a fresh angle or to approach the subject in a new way, can make a huge difference to any task. Our saints can help us and they can show us the way, letting us see what we can accomplish.

So, our heavenly friends, in addition to praying for us and blessing us, also have much to say; they are there to help us on our journey of faith, showing us how to persevere, while leading us onward through the maze of life.

Our saints are people like us, who have managed to stay true to what they believed; they have overcome the distractions, temptations and obstacles to their faith they had to face during their lives and are now in heaven. From there, however, they can offer us words of encouragement, so that we can follow in their footsteps.

What they have to say to us is, maybe, what they said several hundred years ago to others, although their words are just as valid, and just as encouraging today, as they were then. And encouragement is important, especially for those of us who feel tired and worn out by the stresses and strains of life. For many of us, persevering in our faith can be a trial, and then encouragement is most definitely welcome.

St. Perpetua, while she was imprisoned by the Romans, and awaiting death in the Coliseum in Carthage, was constantly having to resist pressure from her family and others to give up her faith. Her call to us therefore (below), to hold firm to it, and to keep safe all that we believe, comes from one who knows all about persevering. Her words belong to the 3rd century and may have been spoken only to her fellow prisoners, yet they are a clarion call to us today, and to all who feel overcome by their doubts and fears and inclined to give everything up.

∫

St. Peter, Apostle (? - 64/68)

"This is a great joy for you, even though for a short time yet you must bear all sorts of trials; so that the worth of your faith, more valuable than gold, which is perishable even if it has been tested by fire, may be proved – to your praise and honour when Jesus Christ is revealed. You have not seen him, yet you love him; and still without seeing him you believe in him and so are already filled with a joy so glorious it cannot be described; and you are sure of the goal of your faith, which is the salvation of your souls.'

∫

Much can be gained from a reading of the two short letters of St. Peter, even though the bare facts of his life are missing. However, there are some facts about him which can be highlighted. He is sometimes thought to be the eldest of the disciples, and according to St. John's Gospel, is the first one Jesus speaks to, which could imply his age or seniority – the two went together in the Jewish culture of the time.

Christ had commanded him, 'Feed my sheep', and in his letters St. Peter does exactly that. He is fortifying and encouraging the faith of the early Church. The letters are very positive: words such as heaven, salvation, grace, joy, mercy, resurrection, blessing, restore, confirm, holy, praise, honour, hope, glory – in fact he ends his first letter saying, 'I write these words to encourage you.' And we can call to mind his words to feel secure in our faith, whenever it is under attack from the pressures and distractions of the world.

§

St. Perpetua (c.180-203)

'Stand fast in the faith, and love one another, all of you!'

∫

Vibia Perpetua was born in Carthage towards the end of the 2nd century. She came from a noble, prosperous family which, however, was disappointed by her decision not only to become a Christian but, in addition, to sacrifice her life for the Christian faith. She was imprisoned by the Emperor Septimius Severus and condemned to death by being thrown into the arena at the Carthaginian Colosseum, and attacked by the wild beasts there. This was despite the fact that she was still nursing her baby, while her servant, Felicity, had actually given birth to her own baby while still in prison.

Perpetua kept a diary of her time in prison and, when the time came for her to be thrown into the arena, she gave her diary to a fellow prisoner, called Saturus. He was to be put to death later on but meanwhile was able to give an eyewitness account of the deaths of Perpetua and Felicity. Their bodies were placed in a tomb and, in the 4th century, a basilica– known as the Basilica Maiorum – was built over the tomb, which still stands today, in Carthage, Tunisia.

§

St. Dominic (1170-1221)

'You are my companion and must walk with me. For if we hold together, no earthly power can withstand us.'

∫

Dominic Guzman was born in the Spanish town of Caleruega, in 1170. He led a strict, austere life, but was also a charismatic, sociable figure, a gentle speaker, and a compassionate listener. Following his ordination at the age of twenty-four, he became a canon of the cathedral of the Spanish town of Osma.

However, it was while travelling on a mission with his bishop, around the year 1206, that he encountered the sect called the Albigensians, or Cathars as they were sometimes known, who taught that all material things were evil, that all people should lead a strict, ascetic life, while their possessions were to be destroyed; sometimes even children were regarded by the Albigensians as possessions and were put to death.

Dominic decided that this dangerous teaching had to be stopped and that he, with a group of companions, would dispute with the Albigensians. He and his friends would show them the errors in their teaching, and would preach the true faith to people. In 1216, this group of companions was formalized into an Order, now known as the Dominicans, by Pope Honorius III. St. Dominic died in 1226 in Bologna.

St. Francis of Assisi (1181/82-1226)

'Let us therefore love God and adore Him with a pure heart and a pure mind.'

§

St. Clare of Assisi (1194-1253)

'This labour of ours is brief, but the reward is eternal; let the noises of the fleeting world and its shadow not confound you.'

∫

'What you hold, may you always hold. What you do may you always do and never abandon. But with swift pace, light step, and unswerving feet, so that even your steps stir up no dust, may you go forward securely, joyfully, and swiftly, on the path of prudent happiness, not believing anything, not agreeing with anything that would dissuade you from this resolution or that would place a stumbling block for you on the way, so that you may offer your vows to the Most High in the pursuit of that perfection to which the Spirit of the Lord has called you.'

St. Anthony of Padua (1195-1231)

'Let us therefore pray to our Lord Jesus Christ that he give us the grace to seek his Kingdom and to build within ourselves a moral Jerusalem. By doing this, we will be able to merit our place in the heavenly Jerusalem, to sing 'Alleluia!' in its streets with all the saints and angels. But the One whose Kingdom is eternal for all ages must help us to do so.'

∫

'We ask you, Lord Jesus Christ, who have ascended to heaven in our human nature from this world to the Father that you draw us after yourself with the cord of your love.'

∫

'Extending his arms on the Cross like wings, Christ embraces all who come to him, sheltering them in his wounds.'

∫

St. Anthony of Padua was a Portuguese Franciscan monk who lived in the early 13th century. People everywhere loved to hear him preach and he became famous for his homilies, for which he seems to have had a special gift. He was also very learned and knowledgeable.

Due to his subsequent fame, stories and legends sprang up about him. According to one of them, his book of psalms was stolen by a renegade monk who had decided to leave the monastery. St. Anthony prayed for the book to be returned. It was indeed returned and the monk who had stolen it went back to the monastery. A large basilica now stands over the place where he was buried.

§

St. Catherine of Siena (1347-1380)

'Embrace Jesus crucified, loving and beloved, and in him you will find true life because he is God made man. Let your heart and your soul burn with the fire of love drawn from Jesus on the Cross.'

∫

'Proclaim the truth and do not be silent through fear.'

∫

'He came to live among us and to guide us home. He will go to any length to seek us, even to being lifted high upon the cross to draw us back to himself. We can only respond by loving God for his love.'

∫

'We are a field where God in his mercy has thrown his seed, that is, the love and affection with which he created us. He gave us the waters of holy baptism so that this seed produces fruit and nourishes the plants.'

§

St. Joan of Arc (1412-1431)

'Courage! Do not fall back!'
In God's name let us go on bravely.'

∫

'Help yourself and God will help you.'

∫

Jeanne d'Arc, or Joan of Arc as she is known in English, was born around the year 1412 in the French village of Domremy. The story of her visions, her short life, her military victories on the way to the coronation of the French King Charles VII at Rheims – these are fairly well-known. So too her trial, the false accusations against her, and her death by being burnt at the stake at the age of nineteen are all widely known. Plays and films have been based on these events.

Less well-known is the gratitude of the inhabitants of the places she liberated from the English, during the Hundred Years' War. In one of the churches in the village of Meung-sur-Loire is a tiny stained-glass window, donated by the women who lived there in 1429; the window carries an inscription in which they thank Joan of Arc for freeing them from the English invaders.

Relatively unknown too is the Trial of Nullification in 1456, which overturned the findings of the former show-trial which had led to her violent death. Instead, this Trial of Nullification restored her good name with the result that she could later be recognised as a saint. Joan of Arc was canonized in 1920 by Pope Benedict XV.

§

St. Catherine of Genoa (C. 1447-1510)

'Believe that no happiness can be found worthy to be compared with that of a soul in Purgatory except that of the saints in Paradise. And day by day this happiness grows as God flows into these souls, more and more as the hindrance to His entrance is consumed. Sin's rust is the hindrance, and the fire burns the rust away so that more and more the soul opens itself up to the divine inflowing.'

∫

Catherine Fieschi was born in 1447 in Genoa. At the age of sixteen, she was married to a nobleman, Giuliano Adorno who, for ten years, made Catherine's life a misery. In 1473 both of them had a powerful experience of God, and worked in the Pammatone Hospital in Genoa, with Catherine, after her husband's death from the plague, becoming the hospital administrator.

However, she is best known for her 'Treatise on Purgatory', which she wrote following one of her mystical experiences. She describes the joy felt by the soul which feels the love in a way it has never known before, and the painful removal of the sins which separate it from God.

For nearly five hundred years her description of Purgatory was ignored, until Pope Benedict XVI, in a general audience in 2011, vindicated her, commending her contribution to modern theological thought.

St. Teresa of Avila (1515-1582)

'The soul's progress does not lie in thinking much but in loving much.'

∫

'Let nothing disturb you;
Let nothing trouble you;
All things are passing,
God never changes.
Patience obtains all things;
Whoever has God lacks nothing.
God alone is enough.'

∫

'The Lord walks among the pots and pans, helping us both inwardly and outwardly.'

∫

Teresa Sanchez de Cepeda was born to a noble family in 1515 in the Spanish city of Avila. At the age of twenty, she entered the Convent of the Incarnation, although she soon found it was rather too relaxed and self-serving and longed for more discipline, solitude, and contemplative prayer in the convent.

For the next twenty years she occupied her time with much reading, intense prayer, mortification of the flesh, and listening to sound advice. Then she began to experience raptures and visions; one in particular is now referred to as the transverberation of the heart.

She describes in her autobiography *The Life of Teresa of Avila by Herself* how she saw in the vision an angel with a lance, and then felt almost unbearable pain as he thrust it into her heart. Then, as the angel drew it out, she felt a tremendous love for God, a love such as she had never known before.

In 1562, renewed by this great love, she left the Convent of the Incarnation and went on to establish the first of many convents that she had been longing for. These new convents would be based on what she saw as authentic Carmelite spirituality, the nuns there would live a life of poverty, in an atmosphere more conducive to contemplative prayer. Afterwards, she founded twelve more of what would become known as Discalced Carmelite convents throughout the length and breadth of Spain.

Teresa recounted her experiences in her *Life*, and *Foundations*, *The Way of Perfection*, addressed to the nuns in her convents, and finally *The Interior Castle*. She died in 1582, in Alba de Tormes.

§

St. John of the Cross (1542-1591)

'The heavier a burden is, the lighter it is when borne for Christ.'

∫

'Live in faith and hope, even though you are in darkness, because it is in these darknesses that God protects the soul.'

§

St. Philip Howard (1557-1595)

'The greater the sufferings for Christ in this world, the greater the glory with Christ in the next.'

[These words, written in Latin, can be seen carved into the wall of his cell in the Beauchamp Tower in the Tower of London].

∫

Philip Howard was born in London in the year 1557. Despite coming from a Catholic family, he became a courtier, and a favourite of the Protestant Elizabeth I – a tricky situation for a Catholic to be in, as this was the beginning of what became known as the 'Penal Times'.

In 1580 he was made Earl of Arundel, but within a few years was having to face accusations that he had been plotting against the Queen. He attempted to flee the country, but was arrested, and subsequently imprisoned in the Tower of London. After several false accusations, including praying for the success of the Spanish Armada, he was condemned to death. However, he was never executed, but simply left to die. He did eventually die in 1595 in the Beauchamp Tower, where he had been imprisoned.

§

St. Francis de Sales (1567-1622)

'Do not wish to be anything but what you are, and try to be that perfectly.'

∫

'We all have a vocation. We believe that God has placed us in this life to fill a special need that no one else can accomplish.'

'It is lovely to be able to love on earth as one loves in heaven, and to learn to love one another in this world as we will eternally in the next. I am not speaking here of the simple love of charity, because we must have this for all people; I am speaking of spiritual friendship, in the ambit of which two, three or more persons exchange devotion, spiritual affections, and truly become one spirit.'

∫

'Do not look forward in fear to the changes and chances of this life; rather, look to them with full confidence that, as they arise, God, to whom you belong, will in His love enable you to profit by them. He has guided you thus far in life, and He will lead you safely through all trials; and when you cannot stand it, God will bury you in His arms. Do not fear what may happen tomorrow; the same everlasting Father who cares for you today will take care of you then and every day. He will either shield you from suffering or will give you unfailing strength to bear it. Be at peace, then, and put aside all anxious thoughts and imaginations. Amen.'

∫

St. Francis de Sales was born to a noble family in south-eastern France, in the town of Thorens, in 1577. He was drawn to a study of theology, though at the time this involved listening to severe and unsettling teachings on predestination and hell. As well as being disturbed by the strict teachings of the Calvinists, he had to face much opposition from his father. However, he was eventually ordained a priest, elected as provost of his diocese and, in 1602, became Bishop of Geneva.

His *Introduction to the Devout Life* was written and intended for lay people as well as just for clergy, which up to then had always been the case. He wrote the book to help people everywhere to understand their faith. He was a courteous, gentle and loving shepherd of his flock, and was respected by those he met for his wisdom and learning.

Together with the widowed Baroness Jane de Chantal, he founded an order of contemplative nuns, who would receive into their convent all those refused by other convents, and who had been told that they would be unsuited to the austere, strict way of life. This new order, later known as the 'Visitation', would accept the widows, the aged, the poor and the sick and allow them to join the congregation. St. Francis de Sales died in 1622.

§

St. Vincent de Paul (1581-1660)

'It is a ruse of the devil, by which he deceives good people, to induce them to do more than they are able, so that they end up not being able to do anything. The spirit of God urges one gently to do the good that can be done reasonably, so that it may be done perseveringly and for a long time.'

'Let us allow God to act; He brings things to completion when we least expect it.'

∫

Vincent de Paul was born in the village of Pouy in 1581. After being ordained in 1600 at the age of nineteen, he went to study in Rome until in 1609 he was appointed chaplain to the Countess of Gondi. The Congregation of the Missions had its origin there and was involved in work among the poor in Paris. He had been working to help the poor, together with the Company of the Daughters of Charity, a group of well-meaning aristocratic women who were, however, more suited to raising funds to help the poor, rather than actually working among them.

In 1617 he started, with the help of Louise de Marillac, to re-organise them, and recruited young peasant women to do the practical, 'hands-on' work. Thus was born the 'Daughters of Charity of St. Vincent de Paul', now called simply 'The Daughters of Charity.' Vincent died in 1660 in Paris, where he had worked for so long.

§

St. Alphonsus Liguori (1696-1787)

'What does it cost us to say, ''My God help me! Have mercy on me!'' Is there anything easier than this? And this little will suffice to save us if we be diligent in doing it.'

∫

St. Alphonsus Liguori is known today, in parishes and elsewhere, for his meditations on the Stations of the Cross. Everything he wrote and said was with the reader or the listener in mind, so that everyone could understand his words. He could be described as what we nowadays might call a 'people person.'

§

St. Gerard Majella (1726-1755)

'Consider the shortness of time, the length of eternity and reflect on how everything on earth comes to an end and passes by. Of what use is it to lean upon that which cannot give support?'

∫

Gerard Majella was born in 1726 in the Italian village of Muro where, at the age of five, he used to go and pray in a nearby chapel. When he was twelve, he had to find work to support his family. Although each of his employers turned out to have irascible natures and occasionally beat him, he endured it all patiently. He eventually followed his religious vocation and joined the Redemptorists.

As a priest he helped many with their confessions, often gently revealing to them the sins they had trouble confessing. During his life God worked many miracles through him, perhaps the best known one being when he left his handkerchief behind in a house he had just visited. When one of the daughters of the house tried to return it, he replied 'keep it, you may find it useful one day.'

Later on, the same daughter was giving birth to a child, but there were complications and she was in danger of death. Then she remembered the handkerchief and called for it to be brought and placed on her. Immediately the danger passed, and she had a healthy child. Today Gerard Majella is known as the patron saint of childbirth and of mothers-to-be.

St. Elizabeth Ann Seton (1774-1821)

'The accidents of life separate us from our dearest friends, but let us not despair. God is like a looking glass in which souls see each other. The more we are united to Him by love, the nearer we are to those who belong to Him.'

∫

'Live simply, so that all may simply live.'

∫

'All God asks of us is the Heart.'

∫

'Be but faithful to Him with your whole heart, and never fear. He will support, direct, console, and finally crown your dearest hope.'

∫

Elizabeth Ann Bayley was born in 1774 in New York into a socially prominent family. When she was nineteen years old she married a wealthy businessman named William Seton. She engaged in work in her neighbourhood, looking after the sick and the dying, while maintaining her social standing and enjoying a prosperous family life.

This, however, ended abruptly when her husband went bankrupt and then, shortly afterwards, died of tuberculosis. Elizabeth began to look for a way to support herself and her five children, eventually setting up an academy for young ladies. A few years later she moved to Emmitsburg in Maryland, where she established the Sisters of Charity of St. Joseph, dedicated to the care of children from poor families and providing free education for them. She died in 1821, and is often called the patron saint of widows.

§

St. Damien of Molokai 1840-1889)

'We must choose the state God has predestined for us, so as to be happy in our next life.'

∫

'Turn all your thoughts and aspirations towards heaven. Work hard to secure for yourself a place there forever.'

∫

Jozef de Veuster was born in the village of Tremelo in Belgium. At the beginning of 1859 he joined the Congregation of the Sacred Hearts of Jesus and Mary, taking the name of Damien. Curiously perhaps, he was only ordained as a priest after he had been sent on a mission to what, in the 19th century, was known as the Kingdom of Hawaii. The ordination took place in the Cathedral of Our Lady of Peace in Honolulu, the mother church of the Hawaiian Islands.

His mission was to bring Christianity to Hawaii, and that mission seems to have become for him a labour of love. He applied himself to the building of schools, hospitals, roads, even a reservoir, and all that needed to be done for the people. He became internationally famous during his lifetime, even being awarded a medal by a visiting princess.

He is named after the Hawaiian island of Molokai, where he worked among the lepers. He cared for them, dressed their wounds, ate and drank with them and shared their way of life. After a time though, he contracted leprosy himself but insisted on staying with the lepers and working for them for as long as he could, eventually dying at the age of forty-nine, on the island of Molokai. His tomb can be found at the Church of the Congregation of the Sacred Hearts in Louvain, Belgium.

§

St. Bernadette (1844-1879)

'For the greater glory of God, the important thing is not to do many things, but to do all things well.'

∫

St. Bernadette came to the attention of the world when, as a fourteen-year-old girl she reported to her parish priest that a lady had appeared to her. All that Bernadette told him, over the course of sixteen days, convinced him that it could only have been Our Lady whom Bernadette had seen. Bernadette herself probably never thought that Lourdes would become a place of healing, and that people from all over the world would travel there to drink, or bathe in, the waters from the miraculous spring which Our Lady had revealed to her. Bernadette later joined the Sisters of Charity at their convent in Nevers where, after eleven years, she died at the age of thirty-five.

§

St. Katharine Drexel (1858-1955)

'If we wish to serve God and love our neighbour well, we must manifest our joy in the service we render to Him and to them. Let us open wide our hearts. It is joy which invites us. Press forward and fear nothing.'

∫

'There is nothing little in what is done for God.'

∫

'Peacefully do at each moment what at that moment ought to be done. If we do what each moment requires, we will eventually complete God's plan, whatever it is. We can trust God to take care of the master plan when we take care of the details.'

∫

Catherine Mary Drexel was born in Philadelphia in 1858. Her mother died a few weeks after her birth, but when her father remarried she spent much of her early life working with her stepmother distributing food, clothing, and other items to the poor.

However, at the age of twenty-five, she became particularly aware of the plight of the Native Americans and African Americans, and at the age of thirty-three her ministry to them began in earnest. In the same year she founded 'The Blessed Sacrament Sisters for Indians and Coloured People', which later changed its name to simply 'Sisters of the Blessed Sacrament'. Mother Katharine, as she was now known, established missions among the Native Americans and African Americans, and built schools for them in the south-western states of the USA; she also published a Navajo-English *Catechism*, later on in her life. She died aged ninety-six, in 1955.

§

St. Elizabeth of the Trinity (1880-1906)

'Let us live with God as with a friend, let us make our faith a living faith in order to be in communion with him through everything, for that is what makes saints.'

§

Pope St. John XXIII (1881-1963)

'Consult not your fears but your hopes and your dreams. Think not about your frustrations, but about your unfulfilled potential. Concern yourself not with what you tried and failed in, but with what it is still possible for you to do.'

∫

Angelo Roncalli was born in Sotto la Monte in 1881. He was ordained in 1904, and during WWII he did much to help refugees fleeing from the Germans. In 1958 he was elected Pope, taking the name of John. The election was a complete surprise. Some thought he was too old, and he was called by them 'the stop-gap pope.'

How wrong they were! During his short pontificate he made history by calling the Second Vatican Council. His aim was to make the Church more outward-looking, and he wanted also to emphasise its pastoral role. He was keen on the idea of unity in the Church and reached out to the Orthodox and Anglican Churches. Some of his aims were realised later, although he did not live to see them himself.

He visited prisoners, and at special events young people were able to see him and talk to him. 'Good Pope John', as he was called later on, died in 1963, halfway through the Vatican Council he had initiated the previous year.

Our Saints Help Us To Pray

THERE ARE NO rules when it comes to prayer, and it is perfectly possible to pray directly to God. In the Gospels the disciples ask Jesus to teach them how to pray and Jesus tells them. He adds that they are to go into their private room to pray, though always remembering their fellow Christians, and for this reason they were to address God as 'Our Father' rather than 'My Father.'

Meanwhile there are other ways of praying that Jesus taught his disciples. To take just two examples from St. Luke's Gospel: there is persistent prayer – the 'seek and you will find' prayer (Luke 11: 9-13), which is familiar to many. There is, too, what might be called the prayer of humility, also widely known. It is to be found in the account of the Pharisee, whose prayer was mainly about himself, and the tax collector, who was asking for God's mercy and forgiveness. (Luke 18:6-14).

There are, of course, the printed prayers, such as those printed on the back of prayer cards or found in prayer books. The prayer of St. Francis of Assisi, 'Lord, make me a channel of your peace', provides an example of such prayers. These printed prayers can teach us to pray, and to pray from the heart. They provide an insight, too, into the heart of whoever wrote the prayer, however long ago that might have been.

It is highly unlikely that St. Francis just sat down and put pen to paper. It is more probable that looked sadly at all the hatred, despair and greed he saw round him, and asked the Lord what he could do about it. Then, perhaps, the Holy Spirit dropped into his mind the words '..Where there is hatred, let me sow love'. And the other words just flowed from there. But that is only a suggestion of what might have happened.

Finally, it is good to be able to share the faith and the prayers of those who lived hundreds of years before us. Their expressions of longing found in, for instance, the *Book of Psalms*, can be an inspiration to us. The words 'like the deer that yearns for running streams, so my soul is yearning for you my God', from Psalm 41, are ones we can make our own, and might sound as though they were composed in recent times – yet they were written by people living thousands of years ago.

It often helps when people tell us the way they themselves pray. It is rather like discovering a new town: there is nothing to prevent us from plunging straight in, except that we may not then know which street to go down, or what direction we need. It is useful, and probably wise, to find someone who can be our guide.

It is like that with prayer, and a great deal can be learnt from those who have spent much of their lives in prayer. It also makes things easier and, in the following pages, our saints have plenty to tell us about effective ways of praying.

St. Benedict (480- 576)

'Prayer should be brief and pure, unless it be prolonged by an inspiration of divine grace.'

∫

'Let us realise that we shall be heard not in much speaking, but in purity of heart and in compunction and tears.'

§

St. Clare of Assisi (1194-1253)

'Place your mind before the mirror of eternity! Place your soul in the brilliance of glory! Place your heart in the figure of the divine substance! And transform your whole being into the image of the Godhead itself through contemplation! So that you too may feel what His friends feel as they taste the hidden sweetness which God Himself has reserved from the beginning for those who love Him'.

§

St Catherine of Siena (1347-1380)

'Holy Spirit, come into my heart, and in your power draw it to you.'

∫

'If your prayer abounds in battles of all kinds, in darkness and in great confusion of mind, with the devil suggesting that your prayer is not pleasing to God, we must not give up prayer on this account. Persist with fortitude and unfailing perseverance, realising that this is the devil's way of enticing us away from our mother, prayer; and that God permits this to test in us our fortitude and constancy.

In the struggles and darkness, we may know our own nothingness, while in the goodwill that we perceive in ourselves we know the goodness of God, who gives and upholds our good and holy desires, and will not refuse this gift to those who ask him.'

St. Teresa of Avila (1515-1582)

'Contemplative prayer in my opinion is nothing other than an intimate sharing between friends. It means frequently taking time to be alone with Him whom we know loves us.'

∫

'There is no need to go all the way to heaven in order to speak with one's Eternal Father or to find delight in him. Nor is there any need to shout. He always hears us, however, softly we speak.'

§

St. Louise de Marillac (1591-1660)

'Tell me: with whom do we speak when we pray?'
'With God, whom we call our Father.'
'How should we speak with God?'
'With honour, respect, and love.'
'How should we pray?'
'We should pronounce the words softly without moving our head from one side to another and we should only think about God.'
'In what way should we speak to God as our Father?'
'We should speak to God with great love, knowing that he will give us whatever we ask for ... God has promised to do this.'

∫

Louise de Marillac was born in Paris in 1591. When she was in her early twenties, she joined with the 'Ladies of Charity' in her local church. The work of these aristocratic ladies was intended give help to the poor and downtrodden in society. However, their help was mainly limited to raising funds, and distributing food and clothing. Important as this was, they were not suited to actually living among the poor, discovering their needs and nursing them. Louise had earlier met Vincent de Paul so in 1633, together with him, she founded 'The Daughters of Charity', made up of young women who were more fitted to the practical side of serving the poor. Their activities soon spread and included everything from caring for the sick in the hospitals and working in schools to visiting prisons and tending wounded soldiers on the battlefields. After all she had accomplished, Louise died in 1660.

§

St. Alphonsus Liguori (1696-1787)

'Bear well in mind that you have neither friend, nor brother, nor father, nor mother, nor spouse, nor lover, who loves you more than God.'

∫

'When we hear people talk of riches, honours and amusements of the world, let us remember that all things have an end, and let us then say: 'My God, I wish for You alone and nothing more.'

∫

'Withdraw yourself from people and spend at least an quarter of an hour, or a half-hour, in some church in the presence of the Blessed Sacrament. Taste and see how sweet is the Lord, and you will learn from your own experience how many graces this will bring you.'

§

St. John Bosco (1815-1888)

'Do you want the Lord to give you many graces? Visit him often. Do you want him to give you few graces? Visit him rarely. Do you want the devil to attack you? Visit Jesus in the Blessed Sacrament rarely. Do you want him to flee from you? Visit Jesus often. Do you want to conquer the devil? Take refuge often at the feet of Jesus. Do you want to be conquered by the devil? Forget about Jesus. My dear ones, the Visit to the Blessed Sacrament is an extremely necessary way to conquer the devil. Therefore go often to visit Jesus and the devil will not come out victorious against you.'

∫

John Bosco was born in 1815 in the town of Castelnuovo d'Asti in Sardinia. He dedicated his life to the care of young boys and girls who came either orphaned or from poor families. He would arrange for the younger ones to be educated, and when they left school he would find them work, always ensuring that their employment contract would allow them to continue in the practice of their faith. He founded the Salesians of Don Bosco (SDB) to carry on this work. He also founded an institute which was, initially, for the education of girls but later became 'The Salesian Sisters of Don Bosco.'

When he was sixty-two, he published *The Salesian Preventive System*, which advocated the method of teaching based on reason, religion and loving kindness. It was called 'Preventive' as the aim was, literally, to prevent the disadvantaged young people from ending up in prison or leading a life of crime, which is what had often happened beforehand. Don Bosco, as he came to be called by everyone who knew him or worked with him, died in 1888.

§

St. Damien of Molokai (1840-1889)

'**Be not afraid then in your solitary conversations, to tell Him of your miseries, your fears, your worries, of those who are dear to you, of your projects, and of your hopes. Do so with confidence and with an open heart.**'

§

St. Therese of Lisieux (1873-1897)

'**In times of aridity when I am incapable of praying, of practising virtue, I seek little opportunities, mere trifles, to give pleasure to Jesus; for instance a smile, a pleasant word when inclined to be silent and to show weariness. If I find no opportunities, I at least tell Him again and again that I love Him; that is not difficult and it keeps alive the fire in my heart. Even though this fire of love might seem extinct I would still throw little straws upon the embers and I am certain it would rekindle.**'

∫

'I say very simply to God what I wish to say, without composing beautiful sentences, and he always understands me. For me, prayer is an aspiration of the heart, it is a simple glance directed to heaven, it is a cry of gratitude and, love in the midst of trial as well as joy; finally it is something great, supernatural, which expands my soul and unites me to Jesus.'

∫

Therese Martin was born and baptised in the French town of Alencon in 1873. When she was fifteen, she implored her bishop to allow her to enter the nearby Carmelite convent. He told her she would have to wait a year before doing so.

That same year, when her father took her to Rome, she begged the pope himself to let her enter the Carmelite convent at fifteen years, even though it was before girls were usually allowed to. She was eventually given permission to do this. Despite the austere life and the strict rules of the convent, she showed kindness to the other nuns, who were not always grateful for all that Therese did for them. However, her patient, gentle nature overcame all the difficulties she encountered, and she persevered in her chosen vocation.

The letters, poems, prayers, and the plays that she wrote all bear witness to the simple, trusting attitude to the faith that she had, in contrast to the doom-laden, forbidding sermons of the time, which conveyed the idea of a remote and angry God. The memory of her experience as a child formed the basis of her famous 'Little Way'. She remembered going up and down in a hotel lift and began to think of being raised up in a similar way to heaven in the arms of Jesus. She describes in her book *Story of a Soul* the simplicity and trust which defines her Little Way of confidence and love. She died in 1897, aged twenty-four.

St. Elizabeth of the Trinity (1880-1906)

'You must build a little cell within your soul, as I do. Remember that God is there and enter it from time to time; when you feel nervous or you are unhappy, quickly seek refuge there and tell the Master all about it. Ah, if you got to know him a little, prayer would not bore you anymore; to me it seems to be rest, relaxation. We come quite simply to the one we love, stay close to him like little child in the arms of its mother, and we let our heart go.'

§

St. Maximilian Kolbe (1894-1941)

'Our dependence on Mary is greater than we can imagine. We receive all graces, absolutely all of them, from God through the Immaculate, who is our universal mediatrix with Jesus.'

∫

'One can go to Our Lord Jesus or the Most Holy Trinity directly, not excluding, however, the most holy Mother, for to tend toward God without Mary, if it is with an express exclusion of her, is pride and something diabolical, and the essence of sin is always pride, that is, non-conformity with the will of God; and the will of God is this, that we go to Him by this road, that is, through the most holy Mother.'

∫

'Different prayers and formulas are good and beautiful, but the essential thing is the simple relationship of a child to its mother, this sense of our need for this mother, the conviction that without her we can do nothing.'

∫

Rajmund Kolbe was born in 1894, in Zdunska Wola in Poland. Following a vision of the Blessed Virgin Mary which he received when he was twelve, he joined the Conventual Franciscans, taking the name Maximilian. In 1917, in response to a demonstration by the Freemasons, in front of the Vatican, he formed the 'Militia Immaculatae', or 'Army of the Immaculate.' The work of his militia would be to pray for the conversion of Freemasons and other enemies of the Church.

During the years between the two world wars, he became engaged in establishing in Poland a religious publishing centre and later a radio station. as well as working on the missions in Asia; these included setting up a Franciscan monastery, still standing today, on a mountainside outside Nagasaki. In 1941 he was arrested and shortly afterwards sent to the concentration camp at Auschwitz. While there, he volunteered to take the place of a fellow prisoner who had been condemned to death. On August 14 that same year, he was killed by the Nazi authorities.

§

St. Faustina (1905-1938)

'Oh if only the suffering soul knew how it is loved by God, it would die of joy and excess of happiness! Some day we will know the value of suffering, but then we will no longer be able to suffer. The present moment is ours.'

Silent Saints

ACTIONS SPEAK LOUDER than words, as the saying goes, and this definitely applies to the early saints and martyrs. There are many silent saints, who have never given any verbal message or, as far as anyone knows, left anything in writing, although they can tell us much simply by what they did.

The most well-known must be St. Joseph. The messages most saints have for our lives come from what they said or wrote. On the other hand, the legacy that St. Joseph has left for us comes from what he experienced and from what he did, so we can learn from him.

There are, of course, other silent saints. The few mentioned here can be seen as a cross-section of all those who lived and died for Christ during the first centuries of the church. There are, too, some who are not entirely silent, but still only spoke a few words in the Gospels. Yet despite this, they have had an impact on the life of faith of people down the centuries.

We do not know what they said, but we do know what they did; their actions have been recorded and have much to say to us. So let us look at a few of them, as there are lessons that can be drawn from them, even though they did not say anything.

§

St. Joseph

Perhaps St. Joseph should be mentioned first, although he deserves to have an entire book to himself, as he has so much to say to us.

In our day, we can read at length all about what St. Joseph did and we can learn a lot from a study of his life. Those among us with any questions or doubts about the doctrine of the Church can compare ourselves with St. Joseph who, during his life on earth, was himself confronted by questions and doubts – and overcoming them was much harder for him than for us. We can take our time, while he himself had only a few short minutes, to absorb deep theological mysteries.

It all came about during a dream that God sent him, when his whole way of life was transformed. In the earliest mention of Joseph in the gospels, he is described as an 'upright man'. He would, therefore, have been assiduous in observing the Jewish Law.

Being betrothed to a young woman should have been for him an occasion for celebration; however, discovering that she was pregnant before they were married was a shock, since he knew that he himself had no connection with the pregnancy. Moreover, according to the prevailing Jewish tradition, he could not afford to be seen with her. His fellow Jews would notice, and there would be trouble. Therefore, the gospels tell us that Joseph made up his mind to quietly divorce the young woman, Mary, to whom he had been betrothed. He seems, though, to have remained calmly in control of the situation, which might otherwise have got out of hand.

What happens next is amazing. One moment he is a respectable member of the Jewish faith, with his life dictated by the Jewish Law. Then he undergoes a sudden change. The gospels tell us that, instead of divorcing her, he was prepared to guide Mary three-hundred miles from Nazareth to Bethlehem, and to find a place for her to give birth to the child she was carrying. And after that, to lead them both another three-hundred miles to Egypt. And then the whole six-hundred miles back to Nazareth. And all the time providing protection for Mary and food for her, for himself, and for the donkey Mary was riding.

So what has happened in between? How has Joseph gone from being the law-abiding Jew, and preparing quietly to separate from the young woman to whom he is betrothed, to becoming the protector of Mary and Jesus?

He has had a dream, but one which must surely be seen as the most dramatic that anyone has ever experienced. It must have caused a seismic shift in his whole belief system. Joseph has had to accept that the one God in whom he always believed in is in fact made up of Three Persons, and that the child whom Mary is carrying in her womb is the second of these Three Persons, the Son of God. So Joseph has had to digest the theology of the Trinity in one go. At the same time, he has needed, of course, to understand the motherhood of Mary. The divinity of the child and the virginity of Mary are the next things he has found himself having to believe. Then there has been the need to realise, in addition to all that has gone before, that the Son of God has come down from heaven to earth, will be given a special name and that he himself is to look after the child. So now he has to recognise the truth of that great mystery, the Incarnation.

Most readers will have no difficulty in accepting these teachings and maybe take them for granted. They are, after all, part of the Christmas story. So the account of the dream should be familiar. On the other hand, even if the dream is familiar, there are still many who find these teachings difficult to include in their life of faith.

Imagining what it was like for Joseph and the dilemma he had to face should be of help to them and perhaps to others. For Joseph himself, though, the dream and all it signified can be described as nothing less than mind-blowing. His dilemma was whether he should stay with what he had always believed, or embrace these new precepts. The angel who spoke to him in that dream must have noticed the dilemma he was faced with: either to believe all he had heard, or to keep to what he knew and seemed safe to him. As if to persuade him, the angel then said to him 'Be not afraid'. Believing can take courage.

The dream did not automatically enable Joseph to immediately understand and accept all that the angel said to him. In the gospels St. Luke relates that Mary was deeply disturbed on hearing the angel speak to her. Later we hear that the shepherds were filled with fear. So surely Joseph would have wondered at what he was being asked to do. He would have wanted to think and pray about it all.

'Be not afraid.' The words must have been a tremendous help to him and were words that he needed to hear. So Joseph managed eventually to absorb all these truths, all that the angel had told him, in the short time available to him. Moreover, as if that was not enough, he had to put his new belief into action.

We can learn from him, although we will probably not have to do that and, like Joseph, walk 1,200 miles from Nazareth to Egypt and back. However, we can, at least, believe what Joseph had to believe. And it is always a good idea to pray to him, asking him to help us.

§

St. Mary Magdalene

The second of these saints who have left nothing in writing for us, but who can encourage us in our faith, is Mary Magdalen. She remains silent throughout the gospels, except for the time when she meets the Risen Christ, exclaiming 'Rabbi!'.

However, she gives us an example of gratitude, hope, discipleship and faithfulness. Gratitude, because of the 'seven devils' which Jesus had cast out of her. We may never know what those 'seven devils' were, but she possibly led a wretched life and may even have been unpopular. Whatever the case, Jesus seems to have turned her life around, and he must have had a place in her heart ever afterwards because of that.

Mary Magdalen presents us with a perfect example of faithfulness and devotion to Jesus. St. John's Gospel describes how, in the midst of despair, she remained at the foot of the Cross for three hours in total darkness, witnessing the death of the one who had done so much for her. And even after the death of Jesus, her devotion continues, as she goes to anoint the body and then, of course, we know what happened next. She met the Risen Jesus and realised that Jesus' incredible promise of eternal life had been shown to be true and her faithfulness was being rewarded.

This willingness to follow Jesus even to the grave, and beyond, speaks to us today as clearly as any words. It strengthens within us the virtue of hope – our hope that we too will die and rise again like Jesus, as long as we follow Him and hold onto our faith, whatever happens.

§

St. John

And then there is St. John. His Gospel is well-known, although in his Gospel he says hardly anything. Once again though, it is what he does that says so much, as it has given the Church one its major devotions.

St. John's own Gospel relates how, at the Last Supper, he was sitting next to Jesus. While doing so, the Gospel continues, John leant against Jesus' breast; it is a detail which may not seem remarkable, especially considering the momentous events which were about to take place. Even so, this description of what might have been a slight movement of his head has had a huge impact on later generations.

It was a few hundred years afterwards that a nun, later known as St. Gertrude the Great, was reflecting on this detail, and realised that John had been in a position to listen to the heart of Jesus, and she began praying to the saint. She asked him, in her prayer, if he had heard the beating of Jesus' heart, and St. John replied 'Yes' and described the sound he heard. This might, at first, sound like a wonderful but fanciful story.

However, several centuries later another nun, in a convent in the French town of Paray-le-Monial, had a similar experience. St. Margaret Mary Alacoque was praying to St. John and also asked him about the time when he was resting his head against the heart of Jesus and she, too, asked him what he had heard. She received no answer until December 27th, the Feast of St. John the Evangelist, when she received the first and greatest of the visions of the Sacred Heart of Jesus. And so began the devotion to the Sacred Heart.

Most of the details in the gospels are there for a purpose, including the smallest movements of the people described, and we can gain a great deal by reflecting on them. So who else is there, what other saints are there, who have something to teach us?

The Early Martyrs

The martyrs of the first few centuries, some of whom became saints, should be mentioned here. What we know about these martyrs is not really important; it is what they did which surely has an impact on our lives. Often, little more than their name has been found, and a palm branch painted on a tile in the catacombs, next to where they were laid to rest. Were they all saints? Some were recognised as saints, but as for the others... who can tell? However, much can be deduced just by keeping in mind the circumstances of their lives, the age they lived in, and the pressures they were under,

A few of the names of these early martyrs are mentioned in the Mass, in Eucharistic Prayer I. Linus, Cletus, Clement and the other men saints whose names have become familiar to us, have had their lives faithfully recorded by those who came after them and who were anxious to preserve their memory. Many of these were the bishops and popes who held the Church together during those early years.

However, the fact that it was only men who had their lives recorded might, at first, seem unfair. The women saints named in the same Eucharistic Prayer – Felicity, Perpetua, Agatha, Lucy, Agnes, Cecilia and Anastasia – did not receive the same treatment, and so for the most part their lives are unknown. Meanwhile, it is only thanks to the diary which St. Perpetua kept while she was in prison, waiting to be thrown to the lions in the Coliseum at Carthage, that we have a first-hand account of the death of the first two women named in the prayer.

Still, the lives of the early women martyrs have gone undocumented, for the most part, compared with those other women saints, who lived in later years, whose memories have been treasured and kept safe in the libraries of monasteries, abbeys and convents throughout the world.

Nevertheless, those early women martyrs are not to be dismissed even though little is known about them, since they have great relevance to our lives. Paradoxically, it is those early, unknown women saints who have as much or even more to say to us than many of the men saints whose lives are recorded in detail, about the way we should live out our lives.

The simple fact that they died for their faith speaks volumes. It tells us that they knew the value of their faith, and realised how precious it was to them. It meant nothing less than eternal life. That faith, therefore, was something they wanted to hold on to, and they were determined to do just that.

Because they held on to it, they are role-models for young people, and many of those early saints and martyrs were young people themselves when they gave their lives to show their love of Christ. Moreover, the promise of eternal life meant more to them than the empty promises of the world. They had that sense of the eternal which, sadly, many people today seem to have lost.

Young women like Perpetua were feisty, brave and courageous. They had to fight hard and persevere on their pilgrim journey through life – life which for them was often all too short. They had to stand up to all who tried to persuade them to give in and follow the way of the world. Often their families would put pressure on them to marry a Roman soldier, or someone who was wealthy but who unfortunately held to pagan beliefs. For some the temptation to let themselves be seduced by the way they saw others living happily was a temptation that was too strong for them. However, others, like Perpetua herself and her companions, saw these pressures and persuasions as obstacles which they could overcome.

Any efforts to make them turn away from their faith threatened to separate them from Christ, from heaven, from eternal life. That, however, was something they could not and would not allow.

$$\int$$

The Co-workers of St. Paul

Perhaps the most touching verses of the New Testament come in St. Paul's letters, written to the different communities of Christians. Especially in the last chapter of his letter to the Romans where he greets, by name, some of the many men and women who have assisted him in his work for the Lord, provided him with lodgings, accompanied him on his journeys, or helped him in any way at all.

Persis, Stachys, Apelles, Aristarchus, and others may not be household names, though they were probably known and loved by many in their day. Some of them may have been declared later to be saints; there was no definite canonization process before the Church was firmly established. They were people like us and it is good that we can identify with them, if we do any work in any way at all for the Church. They have gone before us and led the way.

If, from their place in heaven, they could speak to us, they would have much to say to us, and their words might resemble the following:

'You may be spending long hours everyday, working for the Lord, and so did we, but it will not go unnoticed. You will receive your reward. Your work has a value, however unimportant it may seem to you. Do not be discouraged by the obstacles you face, and the times when you think you have failed, or your hard work has gone unnoticed. Persevere in all that you do and you will find that it has all been worthwhile. You are probably doing things that no one else can do, using talents that you did not know you had. When you spread the word or share your faith, you may never see any result, but you will have planted a seed, begun a work that someone else will finish. Never lose heart!'

§

Index of Saints

Acknowledgements

Thanks are due to the publishers of the books on the saints mentioned here, and for permission to quote from their writings, including excerpts from the following:-

The Diary of St. Faustina. Marians of the Immaculate Conception

The Complete works of St. Teresa of Avila. Institute of Carmelite Studies

The Complete works of St. John of the Cross. Institute of Carmelite Studies.

He is my Heaven: the Life of Elizabeth of the Trinity. by Jennifer Moorcroft. Institute of Carmelite Studies

Story of a Soul by St. Therese of Lisieux. Institute of Carmelite Studies.

Led by the Immaculate, by St. Maximilian Kolbe. Angelus Press

The Art of Loving God by St. Francis de Sales Sophia Institute

Every effort has been made by the author to discover, and seek permission from, the copyright holder of the writings of the saints who are quoted in this book. The writings of all other saints are, or are assumed to be, in the public domain.

BV - #0082 - 261023 - C0 - 210/148/5 - PB - 9781915972002 - Matt Lamination